ON DEMOCRACY
BY SADDAM HUSSEIN

ON DEMOCRACY
BY SADDAM HUSSEIN

Artwork by Paul Chan

ΔΕΣΤΕ

On Democracy by Saddam Hussein

Editor: Paul Chan
Consulting Editor: Karen Marta
Design: Kloepfer - Ramsey
E-book Design: Ian Cheng
Copy Editor: Nell McClister
Production: Dustin Cosentino, Madeline Davis,
Micaela Durand, Elizabeth Karp-Evans

Co-published by:

Deste Foundation for Contemporary Art
11 Filellinon & Emmanouil Pappa Street
N. Ionia 14234, Athens
Tel: +30 210 2758490 / Fax: +30 210 2754862
www.deste.gr

Badlands Unlimited
P.O. Box 320310
Brooklyn, NY 11232
Tel: +1 646 450-6713
Email: operator@badlandsunlimited.com
www.badlandsunlimited.com

Enhanced e-book with multimedia content available on Apple iBooks, Amazon Kindle,
and other e-readers. For more information, visit:
www.badlandsunlimited.com

Distributed in the Americas by:

ARTBOOK | D.A.P.
155 6th Avenue, 2nd Floor
New York, NY 10013
Tel. +1 800 338-BOOK; Fax: +1 212 627-9484
www.artbook.com

Distributed in Europe by:

Buchhandlung Walther König
Ehrenstrasse 4
50672 Köln
order@buchhandlung-walther-koenig.de

Essays adapted from *Saddam Hussein: Selected Works, Volume II: Democracy*
(Baghdad: Dar Al-Ma'mun for Translation and Publishing, 1992).

Printer: Amvrosiou Printing and Graphic Arts

Printed in Greece

ISBN: 978-1-936440-32-0
E-book ISBN: 978-1-936440-14-6

CONTENTS

INTRODUCTION

Jeff Severns Guntzel

The question of democracy is an extremely complicated one. It needs your great concern.

— Saddam Hussein

It was the summer of 1999. I was already running late for the meeting with Saddam Hussein's deputy prime minister and confidant, Tariq Aziz, when I dropped my only tie in the toilet, which, in an act of remarkable foresight, I had just flushed.

My only hope was the Baghdad sun. I fished the tie out and hung it on the back of a balcony chair. Not ten minutes later it was dry, and I was fumbling my way to a Windsor knot.

Also running late were my traveling companions, five Americans with two things in common: each worked for a member of Congress back in Washington, DC, and each suffered from a corresponding sense of self-importance.

I had already been on half a dozen "fact-finding" trips to Iraq with delegations of religious leaders, human-rights activists, and journalists.

I was working for Voices in the Wilderness, an organization founded in 1996 by a loose network of peace activists, many of whom had spent a decade or more following American foreign policy in the most literal sense—witnessing and documenting violence and suffering from Guatemala to Gaza, and returning home to inspire sympathetic Americans to organize for change.

In Iraq, Voices in the Wilderness was working to end the economic sanctions that had been strangling Iraq and Iraqis for close to a decade. The United Nations Security Council had voted to impose the embargo in 1990 as a first step in the effort to drive Iraq's army of war-weary conscripts out of a plundered Kuwait.

It took Operation Desert Storm to do that, of course, but when it was all over, the sanctions were still there. The country was barred from importing anything that might be of use to Hussein's military, which, it turned out, meant anything from chlorine for water treatment to cancer drugs. The goal had become the isolation and containment of Saddam Hussein, but the collateral damage was twenty-five million Iraqis who were not Saddam Hussein.

Under the sanctions, foreign investment came to a screeching halt. The economy tanked. The middle class vanished. Doctors, lawyers, and university professors took to hiring out their personal cars as taxis. The poor became much poorer. Reputable humanitarian organizations reported sharp spikes in illness and death among children under five who were drinking dirty water and turning up in hospitals that lacked the medicines to adequately treat them.

My life in those days was a dizzying cycle of traveling to Iraq, collecting stories of Iraqis living under sanctions, returning home to tell those stories to anybody who would listen, and heading back to Iraq for more. This trip was another fact-finding mission, but it was different. A liberal think tank based in the US had organized the trip and tapped our organization for in-country support. The lawmakers who had sent their aides to Iraq either had reservations about the sanctions or opposed them outright. I was a fixer only; a logistics guy. And it was the first delegation of US government representatives to visit Baghdad in many years.

A sad-eyed fellow I'll call Waleed was the government man tasked with looking after us and, specifically that day, with collecting us and delivering us to our meeting. He was in the lobby watching the elevator doors, which opened every few minutes, spitting out one ambling expedition member at a time. This was not lost on Waleed, who, like me, had been foolish enough to wonder whether maybe this group could be a first step toward saving Iraqis from another decade of being squeezed between a belligerent dictator and his also-belligerent international foes.

Waleed had been my "minder" on each of my trips. We had a rapport. I knew him well enough to laugh when he showed us to the late-'80s-model Mercedes he was driving. I had been in his car before, and this was not his car. It was clear the regime had wanted to dress him up a bit for the American quasi dignitaries.

He usually drove a down-but-never-out Honda, and I had been in it many times. To honk the horn (an empty expression on Baghdad's chaotic streets), he had to touch two exposed wires together. And that Honda stalled like a peace process: often, and just when you thought you were actually getting somewhere.

Waleed had a carefully groomed mustache that rode stiffly atop a permanent nervous half-smile. It was the smile he wore in the lobby that afternoon when he approached me briskly, put his hands to my neck, and refashioned the imperfect Windsor knot on my toilet-tie. "Have you ever done this before?" he asked me.

All together now, we squeezed into the Mercedes. For the overflow, Waleed hailed a cab. If you were watching the Iraq war on your television in 2003, you probably saw the building to which we were heading. It is still standing today, despite taking significant fire from machine guns and worse.

Green zone

The large, red, Brutalist structure with guns on top was imposing. It sat on the opposite bank of the Tigris and upriver a bit from my hotel. I could see it from my balcony when I sat and watched the city at night.

When we arrived, a man met us at an entry to the building, and we followed him inside to a long hallway with a closed door at the end. He went through the door and left us to wait. Waleed was with us still, and he adjusted the knot at my neck again. In that hall, Waleed was standing in the shadow of his regime's upper management. He was middle management at best, though I suspected he was much further down the ladder than that. Whatever the case, he was accountable for us. It was obvious he was terrified that we would make him look a fool. And he was taking it all out on my tie.

The door opened onto a conference room with a large, oblong table. We filed in. Aziz was not there yet, but a crystal ashtray had been placed at the head of the table for his trademark Cuban cigar. We each picked a chair, avoiding the ashtray. There was a microphone in front of each of us. Our hotel rooms had microphones too, but the ones in this room were not the hidden kind, and that was refreshing. I tapped mine, but nothing happened.

After a while, a man who was not Tariq Aziz came in with a tray full of tiny teacups on saucers. His hands

16

trembled as he set the saucers on the table in front of us, one at a time. The trembling didn't seem like a condition; the man seemed legitimately petrified.

Until that point, I had been mostly oblivious to the theater of fear Hussein so masterfully managed in his country. But right at that moment, I felt my throat tighten a bit and my palms start to sweat. It's as if it had only occurred to me right that second that I had never made the acquaintance of a tyrant's right hand.

Finally came Aziz. We all stood to greet him, and he worked his way around the table to shake hands. He started on my side. I wiped my palm on my pant leg and took his hand, which reminded me that he was human. Pressing flesh is a humanizing thing, remarkably so, even when the flesh pressed is the living tissue of an inhuman regime. His hand felt small, but his glasses were as huge and cartoonish as they looked on television, where he often appeared, somewhat convincingly, in character as the regime's good cop. Somebody had described him to me as "the warm face of the regime."

We settled into our seats. One of the aides asked Aziz whether it was a real Cuban he was smoking and if he could have one (Aziz was noncommittal, but sent one to our car as we were piling in after the meeting).

Another aide asked, "When will there be democracy in Iraq?"

Aziz took only a short second to begin his response, speaking on behalf of his president and friend. It took him the better part of ten minutes to finish. He started with Hussein's rise to power, but left out the story of the murderous purge of political foes that marked his inauguration in 1979. Hussein had been president just over a year when he went to war with Iran. That blood folly lasted a decade. A million or more people died in the war, most of them conscripts in the armies. Then came the invasion of Kuwait in 1990 and Operation Desert Storm in 1991. Then the sanctions—not a war fought with armies, but a war just the same. Now here we sat at this meeting, the poorly matched and utterly ineffectual representatives of two warring countries. Aziz ended his time-travel response with "Democracy? We haven't had time for democracy. We've been at war for twenty years."

It's been thirty years of war now. A man from Texas who became president of the United States (after losing the popular vote) tried to bring democracy to Iraq, but only managed to deliver hundreds of thousands of heavily armored Americans and waves of unspeakable terror and chaos. Following the 2003 invasion, Hussein's Baath party was ousted and he was reduced, for a time, to a sort of human pinball in hiding, bouncing from place to place, sinking into and popping out of holes.

The year of the invasion ended with Hussein's capture. A tribunal, appointed by Iraq's interim government, sentenced the deposed dictator to death and he was hanged.

There is a new government in Iraq that better reflects the ethnic and religious demographics of the country, but it has completely failed at achieving a true democracy willing to channel the best aspirations of its people.

Aspiration, of course, can be killed just like its flesh and blood hosts, and even as American declares its war in Iraq over, and the UN sanctions have finally been lifted, Iraqi aspiration must survive the lesser wars of random violence, public corruption, economic desperation, and deep psychic and emotional scarring.

I wonder whether Tariq Aziz ever thinks of that meeting in 1999 from the prison cell in Baghdad that is now his home. If he does, I wonder whether he remembers his comment about democracy. And more to the point, I wonder whether he ever thinks to himself, "I was right."

Because he was right, at least about this: You can't have war and democracy; you must choose between the two. And for thirty years, despite the efforts and aspirations of some people in government and millions of people at the grassroots level, America has been on the side of only war for Iraq.

You may find it disingenuous that Saddam Hussein, the murderous totalitarian, expounds on democracy in Iraq, as he does in the pages that follow. Or you may find it obscene. These speeches, delivered by Hussein in 1977–78—to Iraq's Council of Planning and the Arab Baath Socialist Party—were the musings of a vice president with epic aspirations. By 1979 he was president, his iron fist ungloved. He does not promise democracy in these speeches, and he did not deliver it. Not for lack of time, as Aziz suggested, but for lack of interest. In these speeches, he mostly considers democracy—what is useful to him and what is not. And it is, at times, obscene.

My original copy of Hussein's book of essays was a gag gift, purchased by a dear friend at the book market on Mutanabi Street in Baghdad and presented to me one year after my visit with the congressional aides. Back home it ended up in a box in storage. I rediscovered the book sometime after the Mutanabi market had been destroyed by a suicide bomber in 2007, just a few months after Hussein's hanging. As a gag gift it was funny. Now it is an artifact of an Iraq destroyed, dictator and all, and I find even the darkest of humor elusive.

I haven't been back to Iraq since the weeks after the invasion in 2003. Most of my Iraqi friends fled and haven't been back either. And in the palaces abandoned by Saddam Hussein, there are new politicians with epic ambitions, also considering democracy. I've read their speeches too. They should really put them in a book.

THREE SPEECHES
BY SADDAM HUSSEIN

DEMOCRACY: A SOURCE OF STRENGTH FOR THE INDIVIDUAL AND SOCIETY

Council of Planning
July 10, 1977

Brothers,

Your task and that of your Ministry are among the most important tasks undertaken by any Ministry in this country because they are related to what we and our people cherish most, namely youth and the students in whom the Revolution created a new sense of national and pan-Arab awareness and feelings, a belief in the socialist course, and a sense of responsibility. Such a state should be enhanced. What are then the proper means to deal with a student on a daily basis, whether in school or at home, in a manner that makes his interaction with the new requirements of education elaborate and genuine? I put it frankly: the means and remedies being used in this field have not been encouraging so far.

We do not want the student to learn in a parrot-like manner things related to the Party or the State.

Loyalty to the Party is not only proved through membership or by learning Party slogans. Rather, it is expressed by showing genuine allegiance to the homeland, by carrying out one's duty sincerely, by being very careful with time, and by adherence to the Revolution's program in a sincere, proper, and creative way.

It is true that the Minister of Education is guided by a general line. Yet there are many things and many cases and fields that do not fall within his direct responsibility of follow-up and supervision, especially in the details of implementation when they become the responsibility of the lower departments. Hence, when these departments are active and creative the course of work will continue in the same fashion outlined by the competent minister or determined by the leadership for all departments.

We aspire to make the child a source of enlightenment within the family, which includes his parents and his siblings, so that he may bring about positive changes. He may also teach his family some of the rules of good conduct and respect that are based on the Revolution's concepts, because the school teaches him the benefit and importance of all this. If the father is not acquainted with the rules of new conduct, the student or young pupil will be creating a new style of living. Such a style is linked to the principles of the Arab Baath Socialist Party and its approach to revolutionary change.

The basic principles of the Party are based on two main issues: creating a real national basis, and ending any form of injustice and exploitation with regard to Iraq, as well as putting Iraq within the framework of these two issues, in the service of the objectives of Arab struggle.

If we do not create real patriotism and put an end to injustice and exploitation in Iraq, we will not be able to pass on the Party's principles beyond Iraq and not even within Iraq. Then our calls could end up like the aborted experiences of Third World countries, where the concerned leaders of national changes at the beginning of political changes clamor about nationalism, socialism, and other slogans. However, when for some reason they leave their leading positions, the opposition forces come back and take over control of the state without facing any major obstacles, because the laws prevailing when those changes took place remained as they were, and because the persons in the second positions neither brought about radical changes nor created new and firm revolutionary traditions in society and governmental departments. They come and take over affairs under various names and disguises that are legitimate and common, without causing any serious damage to interests, culture, and traditions.

Accordingly, your task is a difficult one, and the job of a primary school teacher has priority

Untitled

over that of the secondary school teacher. And the latter's has priority over that of the university teacher, because a university teacher receives the students as end products whose educational bases have, to a considerable degree, been shaped. If the end products are corrupt, he will not be able to make a great and essential change. But if they are within the general line, his role will be to develop and improve on the results, putting them within the common context of the Revolution's course and programs. Therefore, you should teach pupils and students the details of daily life, as we said, such as the proper use of knife and fork, table manners, asking their parents' permission before coming into their room or before inviting a friend, the respect of public property (socialist property), and being careful with their money and fighting bourgeois habits. Passing on the Revolution's traditions, customs, and directives through pupils and students to their families and safeguarding them against worn-out habits that are still prevalent in these families is vital and essential. You should not consider these habits bourgeois because the principles of the Arab Baath Socialist Party do not state that whoever eats with his hand is socialist and whoever uses a fork is not a socialist. We want all people to use the fork and spoon even though our families did not teach us how to use them, because using the fork and spoon is proper and more hygienic and economical than eating by hand, and because it is so, we must integrate it into our lifestyle.

The bourgeois attitude is mainly based on exploiting man. As for socialism, it is not equality in hunger, injustice, oppression, and chaos. It is equality in welfare, strength, and freedom, for we don't want our people to remain hungry and backward in order to be called a socialist people. We want self-sufficient, well-off, and socialist all at the same time.

We must make the young learn good habits and adopt them at home, because the homes of many of them do not provide the conditions conducive to proper education. It may seem for some these habits are insignificant: in fact, they are essential and important. They are relevant to one of the secrets of our success in building up the new society, and that is orderliness, whose serious impact is reflected in the application of ideas that are common and valid in building up this society. Discipline teaches us how to appreciate the value and importance of time. It teaches us how to respect a senior and to be kind toward a junior. Discipline also teaches a pupil why, how, and for what purpose anything is used, whether at school, at home, or in the street. All this is part of national education. Discipline teaches him how to sit in the classroom and at the table, not to leave the table before his parents, not to start eating before his parents, etc. This is part of making him an orderly person. We should get the student used to obeying discipline because there are important educational, psychological, and national aspects to that. For this reason and other well-known considerations, we find the student who is used to working under the elaborate obligations of order, when necessary, stands still in the sun with his gun night and day. And when he is called upon to confront an imperialist or hostile force in this hot region he is ready to do it because since childhood he has been used to orderly work and its numerous details, which build up and toughen his patience. If further work details within new contexts crop up he will not be annoyed by them, nor by military life and war, because an image of it has become part of his life and his general upbringing ever since he was a student or a schoolchild.

Therefore, in order not to let the parents dictate their backward ideas at home we must let the child play an enlightening role to chase out backwardness, because some fathers have got away with it for many reasons and factors. Yet we still have the child in our hands and we must make him play an effective and enlightening role within the family during all the hours he spends with the family in order to change his family's lot for the better and keep him away from harmful imitation.

This does not conflict with true loyalty to the family, respect for one's parents, and the family unity that we are after. Family unity should not be based on backward concepts. Rather, it should be based on and consolidated by being in harmony with the central policies and traditions applied by the Revolution in building up the new society. Whenever family unity conflicts with the proposed policies that are applied to build up the new society, this conflict must be solved in favor of the policies and traditions for building up the new society and not vice versa. Our task then is very hard and complicated, and the brush of a competent artist is needed to give the intended image its proper colors. It is easy to use the ḥammer in industry, the axe and the spade in farming, but in education there is no way to apply the method of using the axe, the spade, or the hammer because the whole work sometimes lies in the artist's brush, to ensure the precise image we want to achieve and present as a new model for building up society.

We must be realistic revolutionaries in raising up the new generation accordingly. We should not be surprised at the negative phenomena in society and feel too helpless or confused to treat them. Many of our people, including Party members, have not been able to cast off entirely the old society's concepts and traditions—though they did so in terms of ideology. Casting off a code of conduct is more difficult than casting off ideas, though we assume there is always harmony between thought and behavior. If there has been a considerable tax on ideas mainly consisting of continuous sacrifices and struggle in an early stage, this "tax" has now diminished or has other directions, less serious in their general context at this stage. As for behavior, its tax continues though its form has changed. It is the tax of getting on with others at the expense of particularities that conflict with the course and interest of society. This is expressed in such-and-such terms in the socialist field and such-and-such terms in national education or in the field of Arab struggle, etc. Therefore we believe that harmony of thoughts does not necessarily produce the required image in detail. But it is supposed to lead to the same image in the end. As for the details, we may find some drawbacks, lack of correspondence, or even contradiction. We may find a Baathist who is not at odds with us in understanding socialism, but who dissents when socialism threatens his interests or wishes. When the split comes about and disorder sets in, it will be at the expense of general creativity and not only at the expense of the Arab Baath Socialist Party's principles. Hence we realize that the Party is a school for enhancing immunity. But nationalism is not confined to Party members, nor is loyalty. This case is similar in some aspects to examinations. Is an examination the only criterion that proves the competence of all students? The answer is no. But do we have a criterion other than this? The answer is also no. So we have no way to enhance people's immunity, awareness, belief, and effectiveness, to lead society successfully and to achieve their pronounced national and Arab objectives, other than affiliation to the Party.

Nevertheless, this does not prevent the Arab Baath Socialist Party from stressing that nationalism is not an exclusive right of the Arab Baath Socialist Party, nor is loyalty felt by Party members only. Accordingly and from a realistic revolutionary viewpoint, the Party has emphasized that the Baath Party's formula is not formal. It is a formula of principles and practices related to Baathist principles. Hence, we may say that every citizen who is loyal to the homeland, loves his people and his work, and cares for them and believes in the Revolution is Baathist in his own way.

Brothers, you have done so much, but all the same, we would like you to know that we hope you will contribute yet more because your ambition, which is the Revolution's ambition, is great.

You should win over the adults through their children as well as by other means. Teach the student and the pupil to disapprove of his parents if he heard them talk about the State's secrets, and to inform them that this is wrong. Teach them to criticize their parents politely if they heard them talk about the secrets of Party organizations. You should place in every corner a son devoted to the

Untitled

Revolution, with a reliable eye and a wise mind. He would receive his directives from the Revolution's responsible center and carry them out, store old formulas and treat them in a proper way, psychologically and socially, while he maintains and respects family unity.

Teach him to object politely if he finds one of his parents squandering the State property. He should inform his parent that it is dearer than his own property, because he can't have his own personal property if the State doesn't have its property, and that State property belongs to society. Hence we should be proud of it and be careful with it.

You should also teach the child at this stage to be wary of foreigners, because they act as spies for their countries and some of them are elements of subversion against the Revolution. Therefore befriending a foreigner and talking with him without supervision is not permissible. Instill in him caution against imparting State and Party secrets to a foreigner. He should politely warn others, both young and adult, not to discuss indiscreetly Party and State secrets in the presence of foreigners. In his relationship with the teacher the child is like a piece of crude marble in a sculptor's hand. The teacher can mold him into the required shape and not leave it for time and the elements of nature.

Thus, we are called upon to be in control of the main keys and leave the ends open for the purpose of taking initiatives. We should not leave them loose beyond the central framework of supervision and decision-making in order not to let initiatives be aborted or put an end to the required centralization in planning and supervision. This is one of the Revolution's basic rules in dealing with the movement of building up society not only in this field but also in all other fields.

However hard we try, we always feel that we must work harder, and most of the time we feel there is more to be achieved. Why do we feel so when we have achieved many good things? We feel so because our ambition exceeds our achievements, and because our ambition is renewable. Thus, we sometimes feel as if we haven't achieved something vital or essential, or feel we haven't quite fulfilled our ambition. This feeling is necessary for development and initiative purposes. Nevertheless, what we want is contentment and not despair, that is, self-satisfaction that enhances confidence—but without overlooking the requirements of continuous initiative and development, so that man may not lag behind in his abilities, ideas, and policies.

Avoid being polite at the expense of doing the right thing. If you do so you will succeed and win people's love, though you will face some difficulties. Here as we talk we are well aware of the difficulties in practical life for those who reject hypocrisy, falsehood, and mere talk. We also know that by taking such an action you will face difficulties. Some of you may stumble, may be trapped by others, or may be misunderstood because we know that such things do happen in the Party, the State, and society. Since it could happen in the Party, which is the most homogeneous circle, why shouldn't we expect it to happen in the State and in society, which are less homogeneous than the Party? Society moves in a circle unrelated to the State and the Party. Hence its loose ends allow more freedom because there is less need for laws that control its movement even in its smaller units, compared with the demands of the Party's inner life.

Sustaining some losses is necessary not only as part of the sacrifice and the struggle in the circumstances of the underground stage; we have also to suffer losses as we develop and build up in the course of positive action. The first Iraqi who did away with the veil was the first victim made for the sake of all Iraqi women. The first woman who worked in a factory was the first victim made for the sake of all working women. The same goes for the first woman doctor, first woman lawyer, first real revolutionary, etc.

There are circles whose interests are hurt when dealing out justice and fairness, so they reject them. Yet all people seek and want justice. But when the interests of some people clash with the requirement of justice they strive to make the one who is responsible for applying justice look unjust because their personal case won't be settled in their favor unless that person was actually unjust. Beyond their own case they might very well like justice, but it is their personal case that conflicts with justice and makes them demand that others depart from the course of justice.

Observing justice and fairness is a human duty that is faced with real difficulties in one's home, among friends in the Party or in one's relation with the minister or in the minister's relation with the director-general or the undersecretary. Sometimes one might even reach a stage in his career where he says to himself: "Since people want to depart from justice, why should I continue to be just?" An action such as this is certainly deviation, and it should never be part of our policy or conduct. Rather we should allow for some losses and accept a degree of sacrifice in order that the right and just course may be firmly established, because this is the way of real revolutionaries who believe in the justice of their cause and in their people.

It has been proved by experience that even the people whom you treat severely with justification would first reject you and be annoyed by you, but after a while they will like you. And when severity has nothing to do with personal intent or design to harm, they will accept it however harsh it is. Sometimes they accept some aspect of it even when it is wrong, provided that it is not related to a personal motive or a grudge, and it should not be a consistent policy.

There are many examples of this in our careers. Sometimes we deal harshly with some of our comrades and we fail in doing justice to them. Yet this comrade whom we wronged comes with his grievance to us, we who took such action against him. Such a spirit has proved, by experience, that man deep down wants justice even when it hurts him, because most people benefit from justice and finally achieve their real interest. It's only the minority who reject it. And this is the gain we achieve with time.

Remember, brothers, that any man will find out your personal motive however hard you tried to hide it when you hurt him, because every line in your face will say it and you could never conceal it. Just as truth speaks out from its position, injustice will also cry out. Thus, it will be visible and exposed. No matter how many people you gather around you by propitiation you will inevitably lose them because you did not win them over. I am telling you this from experience and through our work in the Party and in the State. Winning people by propitiation is based on personal gain or personal interests, and personal interests are not necessarily material, because there are personal nonmaterial interests. So rallying people through propitiation and personal interests will inevitably fail as personal interests decrease or clash. Therefore, brothers, try to instill this spirit into everyone and make it part of your concerns.

I notice the development that is going on now and see how the present situation is different from what it was a year or three years ago. Within a year it will be different again. But we will always call for more and work for it. Accordingly, you must awaken the students' and pupils' awareness. Relate your experiences to them and interact with them. Respect their opinions and supervise their affairs carefully and in detail, because they are real specimens whom you must observe and deal with in a lively way. No man should think that he could do without others who are his subordinates, because as soon as he feels so he will be finished. Whatever his degree may be in education or in struggle, he will dry up, because with such an attitude he will cut off the sources of strength and terms and bases of true interaction and development.

There is no contradiction between democracy and legitimate power. No one should ever imagine that democracy would debilitate him or diminish respect for him and his legitimate power, because this is not true.

There is no contradiction between exercising democracy and legitimate central administrative control according to the well-known balance between centralization and democracy. It is only

43

those who are poor in ability and knowledge who imagine that there is a contradiction between democracy and centralization, between care for others and comradely and brotherly treatment, on the one hand, and maintaining the role and position of leadership, on the other.

Democracy consolidates relations among people, and its main strength is respect. The strength that stems from democracy assumes a higher degree of adherence in carrying out orders with great accuracy and zeal. Strength in this case would not be personal but rather a principled and objective attitude. This is the main value of the result of interaction and democratic relations between seniors and juniors. Therefore, be concerned in it because it is a source of real strength for you. All other images of strength are false and are only related to a particular case and time: as soon as they end, the person finds himself unarmed and unable to stand up before the humblest and lowliest people, before the most trivial and least complex situations.

Pay attention to citizens' demands and grievances and do not feel weary or bored by the persistence of these demands, because if you save a wronged person, partially or totally, you will be doing a great service to the people and the principles of your Party. The sense of injustice is a serious thing. There is nothing more dangerous than a human being who feels he is wronged, because he will turn into a huge explosive force when he feels that no one in the State or in society is on his side to redress the injustice. Hence, you must deal with people in a way that pleases God and society and satisfies your Party and Revolution. You should not be afraid of the truth. Bear up even with the unjustified reactions of others for the sake of truth and the great values you hold and strive to establish.

DEMOCRACY: A COMPREHENSIVE CONCEPTION OF LIFE

Council of Planning
July 26, 1977

The question of democracy is an extremely complicated one. It needs your great concern, each from his own position and through correct practices. It is not enough to take care of it theoretically, because our Party is no longer an underground revolutionary movement whose members deal with the citizens, interact with them, or make them aware through techniques already known in underground activity. Rather, principles are now standing the critical test, and are put into practice, which needs a special kind of awareness, care, and suffering. Every one of us should remember that the democratic practice does not come at one level only, as we have mentioned at the beginning of the meeting. It should rather be at two levels, the junior in his relationship with the senior, and the senior in his relationship with the junior, i.e., the senior in his relationship with the junior should believe in and stick to him, in the same way as the junior believes in his relationship with the senior, in democratic practices and applications, not for immediate goals and under immediate circumstances but as one of the basic laws of the Revolution and our Party's principles. Some citizens or Party members mention democracy only when they suffer injustice at the hand of the Party or official departments superior to them. If someone's principles shake in practicing the correct formula of democracy, his relationship with people working with him and those who are lower than him in the Party or in professional ranks, and he does not treat that correctly by returning to democratic formula and means, including collective work, he is neither a true revolutionary nor a true advocate of principles.

Any time, anywhere, a revolutionary person should, besides principled considerations that he should not forget, exchange places, metaphorically, with his juniors. Thus the picture is turned over and he imagines himself in the lower person's shoes. He is the one suffering injustice and not the director-general or the Minister. He is the citizen, not the director-general; he is the Party member in the lowest rank and not the one in the highest rank. He imagines how he can deal with the relationship, how he considers it, from his position as a director-general, with a certain minister; how he suffers, gets annoyed, or revolts when democratic justice is not practiced toward him in the proper way. He has to imagine how he would feel when something wrong is done to him as a result of not practicing democracy, or as a result of practicing democracy in the wrong way between him and his superiors, and how he would stick to that and demand proper ways and means of practicing democracy.

Democracy will remain one of the most difficult issues preoccupying human thought, political thought, and constitutional formula now and in the future, in Iraq and elsewhere, because democracy is a human as well as a major political issue. It is also a central issue in the approach of most systems that adopt democracy and have concern about it in the highest circles of the State as well as other sections, and in the relationship with people and its historic role in building up societies. Take, for example, the information media. They are revolutionary and democratic means for making people aware and open-minded, and also for superiors. In order that the information media carry out their task in a proper way, a great deal of care is needed not only from the person or persons directly in charge of it, but also from all of us. We are required to take good care of the media not to spoil them but guide them, cooperate with them, criticize them when mistakes are made, and provide them with the means of strength and development in order to play their role properly in orientation and supervision. Some Ministers or those lower in rank and responsibility complain of unconstructive criticism unleashed sometimes by certain information media against governmental departments. To start with, I admit that sometimes there are inaccurate and incorrect practices in this field. At the same time, those working in the media repeatedly complain of government departments being indifferent to them and uncooperative with them, sometimes of not being taken seriously, saying that a newspaper correspondent or a journalist is occasionally treated as an opponent or even as a foe when he comes to an office, instead of having the door open for him and being given correct information, so that his criticism of matters will be practiced and objective.

We must expect the media to make such a mistake since criticism is a new practice in Iraq, in government departments, and the people's relationship with the authority. There are in your offices personal tendencies or certain errors you always complain of. Such inaccurate information is sometimes submitted by the Under-Secretary to the Minister; it may be submitted by a director-general, or the head of an establishment to the Minister or to the Under-Secretary; or they may make decisions that are inaccurate or incorrect. Similarly, it is to be expected that a junior correspondent or journalist makes mistakes. Therefore, when we consider matters in this respect, or along this line, our reactions to certain mistakes of the media will certainly be less serious than they are now.

The proper way to make the media sector play its role in surveillance and public awareness is not by rejecting this role or defining it in such a narrow way as to make the task in its correct form almost impossible. Rather it should be put in the right form. And to make the media sector function in the proper form we all have to interact with it positively, faithfully, and assiduously.

Some of our new practices must be accepted by us with a certain number of losses in order to bring them to maturity, particularly on an issue like democracy. We must also accept a certain number of losses in applying democracy, because it is not possible to apply democracy without expecting some minor losses. Such losses should not scare us, because when we look at matters in their final outcome defined by the objective and central means, we will see that what is certainly required from us is marching the practice of democracy, toward the achievement of socialism and toward the struggle for Arab unity.

The democratic issue, as we have always said and as it was mentioned in the Party literature and in the speeches of senior officials, does not eliminate the role or responsibility, defined by law or by the general policy of the head or leadership. It does not eliminate the leading role or its exceptional significance whenever necessary. However, the exception should not become a general rule, a substitute for the practice of democracy. Even though the exception may succeed on occasion.

Also, the question of the right to practice democracy is not defined by special competence. The incompetence, sometimes, of a certain office in practicing democracy should not disrupt the practice of democracy. Rather, more care should be paid to the proper level of awareness and comprehension of democratic practice and the modulation of its formula in order to suit the objective situations, public and private, in society and in the sector. Also, the highest competence and the greatest sacrifice, among people and the Party, should not be a pretext for domination, authoritarianism, or individual practice rather than the collective and more general democratic practices and formula.

To clarify this principle, we ask: Are we, who meet here now, including leaders of the Party and the Revolution, ministers and other technical specialists, equal in competence? Isn't there any difference in competence between us whether in specialization or in politics? The answer is: Yes, there is a difference in awareness and in the technical or political specialization ability. But should we choose the most competent one, politically or technically, in order to carry out, on behalf of us, the task that is required by collective work and within the framework of democratic relations? I don't imagine any one of you would say this is possible, because if we commit such a mistake, we will make a big deviation. So your relationship with the lower ranks should not hinder your practice of and special care for democracy. When you urge people to practice democracy, even when you are more competent than the lower ranks in technical specializations in general politics or in endurance, you should not hesitate to practice democracy when they demand it. It is you in the higher ranks who should ask the lower-rank people to practice with you the democratic within the framework of its formula and its acknowledged collective work and within the acknowledged context of the Revolution.

Why should this principle be taken into account? Why is it stressed although a higher-rank person in certain governmental departments is more competent, in terms of individual evaluation, than many of his colleagues? The answer is that the democratic issue is understood as a question of comprehensive life. It is not only a duty but also a right. Accordingly, we consider every man is required in his own position, to understand life in its entirety rather than merely understanding his own specialization. However totally this man understands life, he will be unable to acquire a full knowledge of life, its intricacies and minute details. But when his potentials meet with other people's potentials, from various angles, specializations, and positions in society, the understanding and solution will be deeper and more comprehensive. On this basis, discussion goes on in the Planning Council, in the State, in the Party, and in the National Front parties, bearing in mind the significance of democratic practice and collective work for its comprehensive requirements in specialization and in knowledge. And also because man is liable to be fascinated with authoritarian work in case supervision and collective work are absent. This will lead to deviation or this or that case.

However, revolutionary understanding of the democratic issue does not, as we have already mentioned, eliminate the leading role or superior capacity in taking its special position, if necessary, provided that they do not go far from the right, permanent, and steady origins in democracy and the formula and spirits of collective work. We should not make the correct special dealing with matters a general law and stick to it and consider it an alternative to democratic practice and respect of collective work.

The Revolution is not achieved by the Arab Baath Socialist Party efforts independent of the role of the people and national forces. I do not say this in order to provoke the sympathy of any one of you. I rather say it with conviction. Every one

Horse without rider

of you, sitting here or staying outside this meeting as a patriot among the Iraqi people and national forces, every one of you has contributed, in one way or another and from one's own position and according to one's own concept, to the weakening of the Arif regime and assumed power on 17–30 July 1968. So every one of you has contributed to the creation of this system, which we all in this place discuss how to develop and how to offer our services to our people through it.

The Arab Baath Socialist Party has a special and exceptional role. It has also the leading initiative in starting the Revolution. For this reason the people and all national forces acknowledged the leading role. Is that enough? Is the leading role enough to make the Arab Baath Socialist Party an unauthoritarian Party? Yes, it is enough.

On this basis, and for other reasons, the Arab Baath Socialist Party did not and should not become an authoritarian Party, because there is no objective justification for that.

Accordingly, the efficiency of every one of you, and the role of you in revolutionary work, in political work, or in building up the State, should not be a pretext or a cause for becoming authoritarian and thus doing away with collective work and democratic practices, regardless of his efficiency and revolutionary contribution to the Revolution, Party, or society.

The Revolution would have broken out even if the Arab Baath Socialist Party had not achieved it, because the people would have created the party and the means to bring it about. But the people would have paid a high price if the Revolution had not broken out at that time and by that means and if the processes did not continue in the same context of the 17–30 July Revolution. Probably its loss would have been historic, including the loss of the historic opportunity that the Arab Baath Socialist Party envisaged with high competence and invested its energies and that of the people in benefitting from it.

Would the Arab Baath Socialist Party have achieved the Revolution if we had not been its leaders at the time and if you had not been present there? The answer is yes. The Arab Baath Socialist Party would have achieved the Revolution even if we had not been its leaders. But would the Party have been able to launch the Revolution on that day, in that particular form and with those negligible losses, and achieved the same results? The answer might be no. But is it not enough that the people, the Party, and the members of the National Front have acknowledged this distinguished leading role? Yes, it is enough.

However, this should not eliminate the significance of collective work and democratic practice.

On this basis, we do not believe that democratic practice and collective work will lessen our role, our position, or the people's respect for us. On the contrary, it will strengthen our role, our position, and the people's respect in the Party and the State and in our relationship with the National Forces and in society.

We should never forget the way and means that brought us to our present position and become preoccupied with its formalities, or with illegitimate and improper ways. We should recall the principles, means, and formula that brought us to our present position.

None of us would have occupied the present position during the Arif regime with its out-of-date values, those of the previous regimes. It is true that some of you, or all of you, are more competent than the average worker, the civil servant, and the junior officer, but we should remember that we have reached our present positions by way of their efforts, or at least the efforts of most of them. We would be unable to keep our present positions unless we remember and take care of the principles that we struggled and revolted for, and unless we continue to care for the people, serve them, each from his own position and in the light of his own responsibility and capacity. So we must not forget them, because the principles and formula that brought us to these positions are the proper course we should always remember to follow in our relationship with other citizens, political forces, and our comrades in general.

If we do not practice democracy, we lose you and we lose ourselves. We lose you, because we will be unable to keep you, however firmly we stick to you, if the people and the Party are not satisfied with you. If we keep you against the people's will and their leader's will, the Arab Baath Socialist Party, we will be able to neither keep ourselves, nor keep our principled and influential position in the Party and the Revolution and in our relation with the masses. And because we do care for you, we sometimes get tough with you and subject you to objective judgment only because we want to make you recognize the significance of collective work practices by democratic practice, and because we want to maintain the essence of the principles we want, at the same time, to retain. Therefore no one of us should be deluded by personal satisfaction if this satisfaction is outside the principles we have just mentioned, because any satisfaction that is not within the principles we have mentioned will be unable to maintain a balance and continuity in later stages.

Remember, as we all must remember when we do our jobs, that a complaint of injustice is closer to heaven by all principles and values, including the principles and values of the Party and the Revolution.

When facing falsehood and deviation, the force of righteousness is turned into a great power. When the wronged person cannot express it with proper accuracy through his own individual effort, others will express it by other means. And it will take its correct course in expressing itself whether by the wronged person or by other people in society.

We hope you won't be bored by people's complaints, because a citizen who does not find someone to complain to about his concerns will look for other means in order to get rid of the state in which he finds himself. Probably an attempt to get rid of the source of injustice will be part of it. Such a feeling may make people fall, unintentionally, into anti-revolutionary activities.

Directive by the Revolution Command Council asking the Ministers to open their doors and listen to people's complaints did not realize the correct forms. We have enough information to meet this, as some Ministers deputize their secretaries to meet the civil servants working in their Ministries or the citizens who complain to them. Others still do not make any real or important contribution whether in this respect or in the other levels of the State.

It is true that dealing with individual cases cannot replace central laws in changing the modes of society in a forward direction and in a revolutionary way. Yet these dealings, or at least some of them, besides the continuous efforts in transforming society by means of total and general central laws, from an important issue now and in the future.

It is a psychological and political issue as well as an important process necessary for every one of us to see part of society's movement through the types of complaints submitted to us, and in order to recognize what one has, or has not, achieved on the path of principles and policies linked to it.

Meet with the people who contact your offices, brothers, and meet with the civil servants working at your offices and respond to them according to proper contexts and procedures. Then you will find that you have benefitted a great deal, because the democratic issue and the practice of authority are not a scholastic issue. It is not like the old-fashioned teacher-student relationship, when a teacher used to come into class, give his lesson, and leave after the students had memorized it. The democratic issue and the practice of power require considerable interaction with people, for while you teach others a lesson, the people lower than you in responsibility will teach you many lessons through various types and through the views they voice from their own positions, and on the basis of their own experience and education.

We are all required to maintain and develop the conscious stimulus created by the Central Symposium on Productivity and other marginal symposiums.

We do not have to turn work and the democratic spirit, created by these symposiums, into formal

63

contexts and formulas as some will do when they prepare a tidy working paper and bring people to discuss its contents in order to approve it afterward. What is required to understand people's general concerns in society and work by inviting them to discuss the issue of production and productivity: listen to their views about the correct things they see in government departments that make them perform tasks in a better way, and interact with their views. Discuss the defects in government departments and in the work of the civil servants, then find the suitable solutions for them.

We must understand in a realistic way that democracy might not be practiced in the correct way by all people. But, as we have said before, there must be some losses. You will sometimes see a deviation from the correct democratic spirit and forms. But we must accept a certain number of losses along with continuous orientation and control and, if necessary, strict calling to account. So we do not have to hesitate and we do not have to deviate from the right path when our march is faced with problems of this nature, because problems that hinder the right path are dealt with by solving them rather than by deviation from the right path. There is a difference between a decision coming to you from a higher rank and a decision of which you are a part, contributing to its making and voicing your views about its formulation while at the same time maintaining your position, authority, and, if necessary, power of decision. Any one of you can practice democracy and at the same time maintain the leading and guiding role required from him, whether he is a Minister or any other officer, whoever he may be. It should not be accepted that anyone puts himself above the Revolution, people, and Party, because they are above us all. Being above us all is something that won't lessen our role or size. On the contrary, it will make us play a greater and more influential role. We must always recall the past and help people to understand it. We must also be faithful to the principles and policies in practice.

The position occupied by the Revolution, the position occupied by the Front, and the position occupied by us in vital areas of the Revolution and the State have not been given to us. They were seized by force, as you know. Remind people of that, but don't be conceited. The relation between you and the people should not be supercilious. And remember that the correct framework of the relation is to be an interactive leadership relation.

DEMOCRACY: A PRINCIPLED AND PRACTICAL NECESSITY

Meeting of Arab Baath
Socialist Party's Regional Leadership
January 29, 1978

The democratic practice is a principled point of departure expressing the Party's unwearied policy and its ideological perceptions, which derive their basic characteristics from the particularity of the Baath ideology and its practical applications. The democratic practice is thus the genuine, principled vision and expression of the people's will and conscience within the framework of sound revolutionary perception, which avoids in its calculations the fall into the illusions of liberal ideas, and defines the spheres of this practice in their proper conscious tracks.

Democracy, in the Arab Baath Socialist Party's view, is of a well-defined revolutionary base deriving its characteristics from its association with our socialist ideology. In its Baathist particularity, it motivates the citizen and the people and reactivates their hidden resources, formerly restricted by depression, deprivation, fear, and hesitation. This active motivation of the citizen's and society's capabilities turns their revolutionary movement into a great force on the path of the revolutionary process and its evolution. Keeping the sources of anxiety and fear in the life of the citizen and the people like a nightmare threatening their life and future will seriously reduce their power to the weakest state possible.

People's democracy, in this sense, is closely related to public opinion that, besides the fact that it is governed by rules and principles, is also based on the principles of submitting to the people's will and respecting the value of the individual. The national political map and the competition among various parties to win public opinion and the Party's pan-Arab responsibility, which stems from its pan-Arab organization and aspirations, lead us to pay more attention to public opinion. Respect for the opinion of the individual along the path we guide him and not the path we are driven to is an urgent practical and political necessity in addition to being a principled duty. The general trends and development taking place in the world are in the interest of democracy. Naturally everything develops in this direction. Interaction with the people's public life and respect of the people's opinion have become a fact, receiving growing attention from peoples of the world. The authorities derive their powers from it.

The citizen has been able to benefit from the world's culture and information. He now can receive any radio broadcast and listen to and watch world television, in line with the development of technology and science. Science and technology have developed to the extent that the citizen can see, through directly transmitted television, the political and social life of the world and learn a great deal. People's awareness, education, and aspirations will expand accordingly.

Democratic practice should be permanently part of our policies as it constitutes a basic part of the Arab Baath Socialist Party's ideology, which considers the individual a high value but not the absolute value: for the outcome of the higher value is not the individual alone as an independent entity, but rather all the interacting central objectives at which our Party aims.

Man, according to the objectives, is a high value among other high values. Man should consequently be respected; sometimes he is underrated. Generally speaking, the less-educated and lower-ranking cadres in the Party are more inclined to underrate others than better-educated and higher-ranking cadres in the Party.

The outcome of the lawyers' election makes it imperative for us to realize that if we were to allow "liberal democracy" in this sector of society, namely to allow all the people, including the anti-Revolution

71

Untitled

elements from the class, political, and ideological point of view, to participate in the elections, or if we were to allow a Baathist democracy, namely people's democracy, by allowing the revolutionary forces only—Baathist and non-Baathist—to try their lot under the Party's leading and guiding role, I think that the winning candidates in the lawyers' elections would not have won in the two above-mentioned democracies. Through the report that we have reviewed, the result, according to my knowledge and calculations, would have been that this list would be defeated while another list would win, whether candidates were Baathists only or Baathists and others who support the Revolution and its march, but they would never be, however, the same people who have actually won. This means there is a defect in two areas: first, in choosing the people in a serious manner, as a real expression of the people's will. Now that we have reached this stage and after completing the tenth year of the Revolution's march, we should bridge the gap between Baathists and non-Baathists in terms of assuming responsibilities, particularly non-leading responsibilities, in the sectors of society or the State at this stage. In practice, we must pay attention to the nature and particularity of each stage to fully implement democracy as we understand it and bridge the gap in terms of assessing loyalty to the country and the Revolution as a serious indicator of a liberated country, people, and society.

If there is still a defect in this regard and if the gap is still wide between the Baathist in his loyalty to the Revolution as was the case in 1970, this means that we have not realized total and vital integration and cohesion with the people.

The expression of loyalty in more precise formulas is a characteristic of the Baathist. In competing with another citizen, the Baathist does not compete in terms of loyalty in its general concept and expression. After a period of time, which we might reach in five years, there will no longer be a large number of people who could be described as class enemies of the Revolution and reactionary enemies of the Revolution. The number of political enemies will also decrease, and they will be of no significance. The appropriate conditions making the people equal in general loyalty and in the bases of general loyalty with the Baathists will be provided. The Baathist is better than a non-Baathist in the ability to express loyalty in more precise terms; when the Baathist is ahead of the non-Baathist in this ability, due to his special preparation and upbringing, he will be ahead of other citizens in the expression of loyalty in terms of the details of the programmed daily work. In the competition in loyalty, ability, and precision of expressing it as a basis for the individual's progress, the Baathist will advance ahead of the other citizens due to the qualities that qualify him to assume leading positions in society and the State.

74

Stemming from this fact, we should endeavor to help our comrades develop themselves scientifically and to develop their potentials so that they can compete with the society that we are part of and compete with other citizens who are also the sons of the Revolution according to legitimate bases. Illegitimate competition developing from unequal opportunities should be ruled out: sometimes an opportunity is provided to a Baathist because of his Party affiliation, which is denied to a non-Baathist citizen. What the Baathist is required to do is to snatch the available opportunity through his qualifications in terms of competence and precise performances in the daily work as an expression of loyalty to the Revolution's policies and the requirements of serving the country and the people, and not through granting the Baathist the opportunity of being preferred to other citizens regardless of his competence and performance.

When there are two ways leading to an opportunity, one of them full of obstacles while the other is straight, and when the Baathist is given the straight way to that opportunity while the other way is given to the non-Baathist citizen, the Baathist will get that opportunity while the other citizen will fail to do so. Accordingly, the Baathist does not occupy a particular position as a result of his "technical, revolutionary" abilities by showing strongly and precisely his loyalty to the Revolution and the Party, but he rather does so only because he is Baathist, while he is equal to the other citizens in the "technical, revolutionary" special conditions in his favor.

A case like this would establish a psychological gap between the people and the Revolution's and the Party's leadership. When a non-Baathist citizen feels that he is loyal to the Revolution and favors the Party and its leadership and is committed to the Revolution's policies, and when he feels that his ability to express the Revolution's course is better than the Baathist who was preferred to him because of being a Baathist, and not because of being more capable than him in terms of the revolutionary and technical aspects of expressing loyalty in a higher and more precise way, then a case like this will harm the people and keep them away from their Revolution and Party.

The second position where we shall lose if this case persists is the one in which a non-Baathist faces this fact and feels that it controls him, so he finds himself inclined to stand against the Revolution and tilts to the opposite trench, i.e., that of the enemies of the people and the Revolution. Basically he is not against the Revolution but against the non-genuine representation of the Revolution by the people who badly represent the Revolution's march and who do not constitute a genuine example.

As I have said, we are in the age of democracy's progress and dissemination in the world. This

explains the Americans' use of the issue of democratic freedoms against the Soviet Union and socialist states through the slogans of human rights and
freedom, although in their general policies in and
outside their country they strike hard at democratic
freedoms and human rights as we understand them.
In line with the sound policies we have outlined, the
other central issue that needs sound frameworks of
action and understanding is the precision and fairness in selecting persons from among the people
loyal to the Revolution and who are equal in the
requirements of general loyalty and from among the
Baathists also. Who are the elements most capable
of representing the Revolution and the Party? We
might be given a list of ten Baathists nominated
to a particular issue and all enjoying the general
conditions of loyalty. We find, however, cases in
which someone enjoying three points in the ability
to represent the Revolution is preferred to a Baathist
enjoying ten points. Someone with two points might
be selected from a group of people enjoying the
same requirements of loyalty, while another one
with twelve points and more capable of representing
the Revolution and the Party is left out. The selection in this case is more personal and temperamental
than an expression of the Revolution's methodology
and principles of justice. This matter makes us lose
the people who are part of us and who want to be
closely attached to us and to the Revolution and

its means in bringing about a radical revolutionary change. It also seriously affects the morale of some Baathists and shakes their principles. Overcoming and doing away with such harmful phenomena that emerge in our revolutionary process obliges us to treat Baathists on equal footing and to express democracy through the high ability of sound selection and with equal opportunities. This also makes us follow a new policy in the Party based on avoiding appointments as a way of filling vacancies in the Party's leading positions and bureaus and on trying not to delay elections at all Party levels below the higher command. This prevents us from filling vacancies through appointments. Appointment is bound to bring a large number of selections under the influence of personal temperament and considerations. A case like this nurtures opportunism and factionalism inside the Party.

When the people freely exercise the process of electing their representatives according to democratic bases every two years, or whenever there are vacancies, their enthusiasm in criticizing mistakes and in building will increase and thus they forge their way into the future through their loyalty to the Party's principles and traditions and through their own abilities. But when they feel that their fate hinges on the direct and personal consent of the Party Branch Members, they will resort to various means to win that consent in a dishonest way.

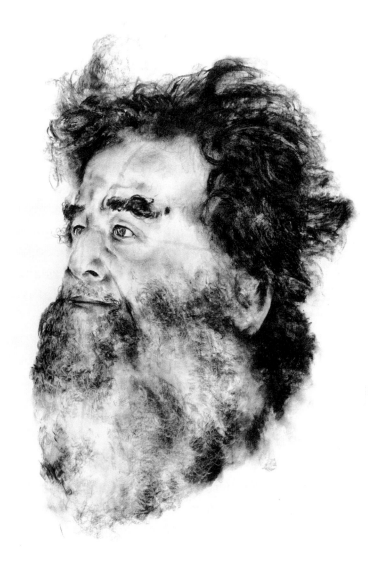

The End

The same applies to the people. If we want to choose five people to the board of the teachers' or lawyers' union out of 100,000 members who are equal in their loyalty to the Revolution, we should not throw the Party's weight arbitrarily behind these five people and neglect the other people. This act will help create a psychological gap between the people and the Revolution. We act upon the consideration that all of them are loyal to the Revolution. This obliges us to help in selecting democratically the required number of Baathists and non-Baathists from among them for a particular purpose. By doing so we gain the 100,000 people and educate people in democratic practices and enthusiasm for the principles of the Revolution under the Party's leading role.

I feel uncomfortable when someone competes with the Arab Baathist Socialist Party in the manner of what happened in the Bar Association. Such a competition is no small matter. There will emerge trends calling for the exercise of democracy outside the Party's leading role in a way that makes others in society, whether social forces or hostile political organizations, call for actually leading the democratic practice in a way that derails it from the path and outside the leading and guiding role of the Arab Baath Socialist Party. Given that, I think that the leadership should pay particular attention to this issue in its policies through high supervision to realize the people's democracy through the Party, namely, through the Party's leading role and in accordance with the program it lays down and not outside it. This will prevent the growth of deviating trends in confronting the state of rigidity and shortcomings in exercising people's democracy, trends that might lead to liberal democracy. A practice of this sort will be anti-revolutionary cover.

Sadat gave nothing of significance to the Egyptian people after he assumed power. He applied a kind of liberal democracy as a substitute for authoritarianism. Had Nasser applied people's democracy, Sadat would not have been able to give something to the Egyptian people on the road to democracy. If Nasser had enabled 95 percent, or any other significant percentage representing the majority of the Egyptian people, to practice people's democracy under his leading role, 5 percent of the people would have been deprived of the exercise of democracy because they were hostile to the Egyptian Revolution and wanted to exercise democracy according to its liberal meaning. When Abdul Nasser died, the 5 percent would have confronted the 95 percent of the people, thus they would have been unable to put forward a program or a call for deviation or something that would lead to it.

With the whole Egyptian people deprived of exercising democracy, the 5 percent had become more capable of expressing the policies they believed in because they were mutually linked by their interests and because they were capable of taking action through their material means of influence. Thus, the 5 percent had influenced a significant proportion of the other 95 percent of the people and formed a cover to the deviations of the post-Nasser Egyptian regime.

To prevent similar things from happening in Iraq, we should not let any significant proportion of our people feel deprived from exercising democracy and other legitimate fundamental rights. This will strengthen and deepen the traditions of the democratic revolutionary process and turn them into a strong barrier in the face of deviations and covers for revisionism. Besides, they will also enhance our people's appreciation of their great Party. By then we will rule out any opportunity of a deviating slogan emerging from the Party or outside it and attracting the majority of the people deprived of democratic practice or any other rights.

This slogan could be used as a cover for certain intentions and deviating policies. In the case of farmers and the election of their representatives, for example, suppose we want ten Baathists in the fifteen-member executive bureau of the General Federation of Farmers' Societies. Let us also suppose that the present bureau has in its membership five non-Baathists while the remaining ten members are Baathists. The latter should be chosen democratically by the Party in the farmers' sector under directions from the leadership and according to the formula it deems appropriate. Their names will then be presented at farmers' conferences for competing with other farmers. This is better than following the selection method, which is influenced mainly by personal motives and considerations, i.e., when someone is brought to the leading positions of the people's democracies. But does the method followed now in choosing representatives of the people's organizations from Party and non-Party cadres express precisely and completely the thinking of the members of the conference as in the genuine democratic way?

The answer is no. The wrong practices pursued in the lawyers' elections are similarly adopted in the elections of workers', farmers', students' and women's organizations. Such wrong practices are also reflected inside the Party while they are practiced outside it in various degrees. The right way is to ask farmers, through a democratic procedure whose bases we lay down, to choose their representatives. Those whose stands are questionable and those affected by the agricultural reform laws should be excluded. This is people's democracy, which means isolating the influence of anti-revolutionary elements on a class basis, and in their political and ideological stands and tendencies, in accordance with appropriate and well-defined formulas and methods and enabling the sons of the Revolution to exercise democracy according to the central conditions laid down by the leadership. But in practice this does not occur in the precise manner we referred to. Why? What happens is that we actually exercise democracy, but we do not exercise it in a precise, sound, serious, and comprehensive manner.

The exercise of people's democracy according to the sound procedures will provide us with the opportunity of using centralization in its precise form against deviations. We do not want the exercise of democracy as a means for escape but rather we want to prepare through it and other considerations the psychological and ideological conditions for the exercise of centralization with an iron will when deviation occurs. By then there will be no opportunity for deviation. When someone is given his full rights, but he does not very carefully carry out his duties, any one of us will have the right to strike with an iron fist against he who deviates from the policies laid down by the Party's leadership or other authorized cadres. When policies are unsteady, giving way to individualist tendencies, the good and evil tendencies will mix in a way that makes people with evil intentions hide themselves behind slogans superficially expressing good intentions while harboring evil and harm against the Revolution. That is what I wanted to say about the results of the Bar Association's elections. As I said, this aberration is not restricted to the lawyers only, but rather it exists in all or most unions in different degrees. It, however, shows more clearly now among the lawyers than others for certain well-known considerations, at the forefront of which is that this sector is full of rightist elements, besides the elements aiming at exercising proper or liberal democracy, which are capable of communicating with us more effectively.

We should understand and behave on the basis that the means we used to strengthen and promote centralization to confront the enemies of the Revolution and consolidate the Party's leading role in the previous years of the Revolution's march cannot go on as they are. We should know precisely the extent of the development achieved by the Revolution and the need for developing and amending procedures and formulas in line with the new conditions and situations, without upsetting the sound balance between centralization and democracy. Developments in every stage of our struggle should be taken into consideration objectively and with revolutionary spirit, without misunderstanding the attitude required when dealing with the people and the need for continuing a cautious and iron-fisted policy with the enemies of the people. We should avoid, however, turning transient phenomena and issues into general laws for Revolution and society.

SADDAM HUSSEIN AND THE STATE AS SCULPTURE

Negar Azimi

In his relationship with the teacher
the child is like a piece of crude marble
in a sculptor's hand.
　　　　　　　　　—Saddam Hussein

The former president of Iraq, Saddam Hussein,
made his public debut in the 1960s as a handsome
twenty-something revolutionary socialist ready to
build up a young Iraqi nation and make battle with
the imperialist ills of the time. He left us, some five
decades later, in a grim execution chamber, hanged
before the eyes of the world. It is a story as old
as Medea and as recently rehearsed as Muammar
Ghaddafi: the man who once proclaimed himself
a modern-day Nebuchadnezzar had fallen on the
heels of an invasion colored red, white, and blue.
Never mind that the world had been misled in
the weeks leading up to the invasion. Never mind
that the climax of victory was diminished by the
interminable military occupation that was to come.
Saddam the state-builder, the architect, and the
narcissist, had lost his ability to frame, script, and

finally color history. Diminished, disempowered, and disgraced, he fell victim to a guard's shaky cell-phone camera lens as he faced execution by hanging. Images of his last minutes on earth — cut, pasted, and rearticulated on countless web sites for the curious eyes of the world — were, in the end, not of his own making.

* * *

Saddam Hussein Abd al-Majid al-Tikriti was born into a Sunni family of shepherds in a village not far from the north-central Iraqi town of Tikrit, in 1937. A law-school dropout, he was twenty when he found his way to the Baath Party, just one year before that revolutionary party would undo a kingly lineage they had inherited care of the British some two decades before. Saddam, whose familial clan was renowned for its cleverness and propensity for violence, swiftly rose through the ranks of the party, overseeing parts of the Baath's impressive array of social services, from work toward the eradication of illiteracy (under Saddam, failure to attend mandatory literacy programs was punishable by jail) to the institution of what would become one of the most sophisticated health-care systems in the Middle East. His efforts went so far as to win him a medal of honor from UNESCO (incidentally, not the first international award he would receive during those years; he would also be honored with the keys to the city of Detroit in 1979).

As Vice-Chairman of the Revolutionary Command Council of the Baath Party from the late 1960s to the early '70s, Saddam grew steadily more involved in Iraq's governance. When the Baath assumed power in 1968, he was at work nationalizing the country's oil interests, modernizing Iraqi agriculture, and crafting foreign policy at large (Iraq, in a sense, was not unlike the Shah's Iran, with its vast and expensive top-down modernization programs). By the late 1970s, Saddam was acting as de facto leader under his aging predecessor, Ahmed Hassan Al Bakr, and, it should be said, was prone to giving lengthy and bombastic speeches on the unlikely subject of democracy. A foretelling of the shape of what was to come, Saddam's speeches were moving and manipulative at once, artfully crafted and characterized by a tone of socialist-inflected egalitarianism. His speeches from this time reveal a leader who commands his countrymen to reject blind allegiance (Do not be a parrot!, he intones), to do everything in their power to eradicate injustice, and to overcome differences for the sake of serving the Iraqi nation (these are, like all good political ideas, riddled with significant caveats). In his speechmaking, Saddam had erected a theater for democracy in which he played both scriptwriter and director. In a 1977 address on the subject of "the individual and society," he went so far as to liken his own job to that of an artist:

> Our task then is very hard and com-
> plicated, and the brush of a competent
> artist is needed to give the intended
> image its proper colors. It is easy to
> use the hammer in industry, the axe
> and the spade in farming, but in edu-
> cation there is no way to apply the
> method of using the axe, the spade, or
> the hammer because the whole work
> sometimes lies in the artist's brush, to
> ensure the precise image we want to
> achieve and present as a new model
> for building up society.[1]

By 1979, the self-styled artist and champion of democratic principles had seized power completely in a
bloodless internal coup, and in July of that year, he
famously convened a conference of Baath leaders at
a conference hall in Baghdad. Dressed in his military
uniform, he announced that there was a conspiracy in their midst, and then sat down. Next, a col-
league slowly and dramatically read the names of the

---

[1] Saddam Hussein, "Democracy: A Source of Strength for the Individual and Society," speech before the Council of Planning, July 10, 1977.

sixty-eight alleged conspirators, pointing them out one by one, for they were all in the room. Twenty-two of the sixty-eight were summarily executed, ushering in a new period of rule under Saddam Hussein. A video camera placed in the back of the conference hall—Saddam's request—captured the entirety of that evening's macabre proceedings.

From the beginning, Saddam Hussein the artist-leader took a special interest in defining the country's cultural production. Under his aegis, the Baath sponsored architectural competitions, poetry conferences, and arts publications, and even launched professional organizations, like the Union of Arab Historians. New newspapers and scholarly journals—for the most part produced by the Ministry of Culture and Information—were launched: *The Arab Intellectual*, *Arab Perspectives*, and *The Iraqi Woman* among them. The latter, which proudly announced that its greatest market was in England and France, exported ideas about Iraqi modernity to the world, and featured articles about women in the military, in the film industry, and beyond. Art magazines, too, were subsidized by the state— including *Gilgamesh*, a glossy cultural magazine featuring articles about architecture, painting, poetry, and photography; and *The International Magazine of Arab Culture*.[2] The Iraqi writer and academic

---

[2] Eric Davis, *Memories of State: Politics, History, and Collective Identity in Modern Iraq* (Berkeley: University of California Press, 2005).

Trenches

Sinan Antoon has written that Baghdad's al-Mirbad festival of poetry was a seminal annual event in the life of Arabic letters.[3] By 1974, a roaming Biennial of Arab Art (launched in Baghdad) was established, and by 1986, the Baghdad Biennial was hosting modern artists from around the world.

Monuments, museums, and historical palaces were erected en masse, too, while the excess oil revenues of the times managed to render these efforts grand—often care of well-paid teams of expatriate engineers, architects, and artists, from Le Corbusier to Frank Lloyd Wright (also like Iran, Iraq became a pleasure palace and experimentation ground for some of the leading architects and artists of the day). Not entirely surprisingly, Saddam the self-portraitist was a champion of the cult of personality, and Iraq under his thumb was characterized by a saturation of public murals, cutouts, portraits, and posters bearing his mustachioed visage. His face and voice were a constant on state-sponsored television and radio, each of which would be gently encouraged to broadcast spontaneous and frequent carnivals of affection for the leader from ordinary Iraqi citizens. His life story was often visually manifest in public frescoes and enacted in day-long passion plays on television. At one point, Saddam commissioned Terence Young, the

---

[3] Sinan Antoon, *Middle East Research and Information Project.*

director of multiple James Bond films, to realize a six-hour telenovela on his life and times.

Historians commissioned by the Baath strained to create seamless links to a glorious past that had been violently and inexplicably ruptured. State-sponsored history writing and cultural production in Iraq came to have multiple uses: discrediting or stigmatizing the histories of minorities it found threatening, erasing histories that were at odds with a tightly circumscribed version of truth, and finally, recognizing the traditions of groups it sought to marginalize by ghettoizing them, relegating them to the realm of the folk museum, the festival, or the performance. Saddam, after all, had inherited a country whose squiggly boundaries had been inscribed by the British after four centuries of Ottoman rule over Arab lands had come to an abrupt end in 1919. In fashioning the new Iraqi nation, the British had brought together three diverse Ottoman-era provinces: Basra, Baghdad, and Mosul. Demographically, the area was made up of Kurds, Shia, Arab Sunnis, Jews, and Assyrians among others. Saddam's task, not to be underestimated, was to create a new and convincing vernacular for this improbable and heterogeneous grouping.

Saddam's *Project for the Rewriting of History* became central to elaborating this state-sponsored narrative, putting forward an entirely novel understanding of Iraqi heritage that centered on

96

the merging of pan-Arabism with an emphasis on an Iraq-centered nationalism that would draw on the country's formidable Mesopotamian history (since the sixth century BCE, this region had been home to multiple empires, variously Achaemenid, Hellenistic, Sassanid, Roman, Mongol, and beyond). A glorious Mesopotamian past, however vaguely defined, was most probably something every Iraqi could relate to, whatever their religious or ethnic constitution happened to be. A narrow pan-Arab and Sunni-centric narrative, too, was promoted to the exclusion of the country's Shia, Kurds, communists, and Iraqi nationalists, who were in turn presented as outsiders, traitors, and threats. Often, these potential antagonists were associated with Iraq's Jewish population, which was portrayed as linked to a nasty pro-Zionist conspiracy.

More and more, the regime hosted leading Arab intellectuals at events that highlighted Iraq's civilizational heritage, while archaeology in particular was put in the service of the state. The historian Eric Davis has written at length about expeditions and digs that were generously subsidized, especially those that linked Saddam to iconic Mesopotamian personalities such as the Babylonian ruler Nebuchadnezzar, who, among other things, sent the Jews into exile in Egypt, built sumptuous hanging gardens, conquered Jerusalem, and, much later, inspired the name of a futuristic vessel in the film *The Matrix*. Saddam was known to fancy himself a sort of contemporary Nebuchadnezzar, going so far as to reconstruct his 5,000-year-old palace on the banks of the Al-Hilla River. New Babylon was fashioned from ochre-colored bricks that resembled Legos, and while Nebuchadnezzar had left instructions in cuneiform script on clay tablets in his palace, and had bricks in the walls inscribed with the pronouncement "Nebuchadnezzar, King of Babylon from far sea to far sea," Saddam had the phrase "Rebuilt in the era of the leader Saddam Hussein" inscribed on each brick in the new version.[4] The palace grounds, which also boasted an imitation processional Ishtar gate (only half the size of the original), swiftly became a favorite destination for Iraqis to visit on the weekends.

While he did a great deal to promote a tradition of literary and cultural production, Saddam banned the four-volume work *Tribes of Iraq* in his attempt to mitigate any sense of tribal identity or difference. In its place, he promoted folk-life through poetry and film festivals, convinced that folklore could unite all Iraqis, providing them with a semi-unified character. As a Sunni, he went to great lengths to address the Shia, who greatly outnumbered the minority Sunnis. Under the Baath, Shia were encouraged to renounce their identity entirely. When during

---

[4] Kanan Makiya, *The Monument: Art and Vulgarity in Saddam Hussein's Iraq* (London: I. B. Tauris, 1991), 71.

the Iran-Iraq War, the country confronted a Shia enemy in the form of neighboring Iran, Saddam tended to invoke historic battles—most notably the defeat of the Persians by the Arabs in the Battle of Qadisiya in 637 CE—that would only confirm a perception of the Shia as mortal enemies. That historic seventh-century battle would be reenacted on Iraqi television time and again.

At least nine new museums were erected under Saddam's patronage between 1968 and 1977. Many of these lionized the struggle of the Baath against the monarchy, while also demonstrating the party's populist character—perhaps especially given the continued strength of the opposition Iraqi Communist Party. The year 1972, for example, witnessed the opening of the House of Popular Culture (Dar al-Turath al-Sha'bi), which both emphasized lost traditions and invented new ones along the way. Among the House's activities was the weaving of traditional rugs, for example, many of them characterized by hokey Baath Party symbolism.[5] A Museum of Costumes was renovated, too, and countless other museums devoted to folk culture were inaugurated around the country.

Like museum collections, monuments could crystallize in built form certain political truths. Artists die, legacies may be subject to the whims of time and

---

[5] Davis, *Memories of State*, 99.

shifts in collective memory, but monuments, for the most part, endure. In the 1980s in particular, as war with Iran raged on, Saddam built many monuments, one more ambitious than the next. The Unknown Soldier Monument, for example, was designed by the noted Iraqi sculptor Khalid Al Rahal, completed in 1982, and seemed to evoke a tilted traditional battle shield, or *dira'a*, possibly falling from the hands of an Iraqi warrior (from just about every vantage point, this monument approximates a flying saucer). There is, too, the Monument to the Martyrs of Saddam's Qadisiya, designed by the artist Ismail Fattah in 1983, which looked like a massive onion that had been sliced in two (it was breathtaking in sight and scope). This latter monument was so ambitious in scale that it was outsourced to the Mitsubishi Corporation for construction.

And finally, in 1988, a series of 100 life-size statues were erected in the coastal city of Basra, memorializing the victims of the Iran-Iraq War and looking out onto the contested Shatt Al Arab strait over which that grueling war (among the most deadly of the twentieth century) was ostensibly fought. Each statue, dressed in combat gear or plainclothes, has the peculiar distinction of having its arms outstretched, pointing accusingly at the not-so-distant Iranian shore. During these years, at least one prominent Japanese architectural journal compared the building efforts in Saddam's Iraq to

The End 2

Haussmannian Paris under Napoleon III. Another writer referred to Baghdad during those years as "one big construction site."[6]

Perhaps nothing captured Saddam's masterful deployment of visual culture in the service of scripting a collective mythology, however, more than a monument that he was said to have conceived and sketched out himself, and has come to be known as the Victory Arch. Commissioned in 1985 — when a "victory" in the ongoing war with Iran was far from within reach, much less realized — the monument took the form of two huge arms holding clashing swords. Reaching a height of forty meters from the ground, the Victory Arch surpassed the Arc de Triomphe or Hitler's triumphal arch in scale and was spread out over what were to be ceremonial parade grounds. As Kanan Makiya details in his masterful study of that public sculpture, *The Monument*, the maquette for the Victory Arch was fashioned from plaster casts of Saddam's actual arms—complete with all the attendant bumps, wrinkles, and irregularities a human arm would have. Adding to the creepy idiosyncrasy of the effort, 5,000 Iranian helmets collected from the front were strewn around the base of each arm. The raw steel to make the swords came from melted-down artillery from the front, too. As if

---

[6] Makiya, *The Monument*, 27.

102

that were not enough, the arches are built in duplicate, marking opposite ends of a parade ground that Saddam would ride through — usually atop a white stallion, which was itself a symbol drawn from Shia mythology (while denigrating the Shia, Saddam was not above co-opting their icons).

Makiya, himself an Iraqi exile with a vexed relationship to Saddam and whose father had once been an architect in service of the regime, has argued forcefully that in his attempt to carve a space for heritage (*turath*), Saddam had butchered it. About the fact that Saddam had erected two sets of arches, for example, he writes: "The duality does not correspond to classical principles of planning in this part of the world; the individual three-dimensional gateway is a vital element of both Mesopotamian and Islamic architecture."[7] Like the twin arches or the rearticulated palace of Nebuchadnezzar or the Sunni leader perched atop the white horse, there are plenty of other examples of Saddam taking historical liberties amid his cultural projects. His construction of "old-style" homes in the Kadhimiyya and al-Gailani districts of Baghdad, for example, were born of designs that had no precedent in Iraqi history, and even boasted decidedly modern accoutrements, like underground parking lots and solar panels.

----

[7] Ibid., 50.

Sometimes, the historical verged on kitsch; the sculptor Mohamed Ghani, for example, was commissioned by Saddam to create likenesses of Alladin's genie and Sindbad the sailor in the form of public sculptures. Similarly, the Babylon Hotel in Baghdad was marked by an entrance that seemed to represent a Disneyland conception of what the Ishtar Gate would have looked like some 3,000 years ago. With all these projects and more, Saddam radiated a will to manipulate the past, to ritualize and formalize ways of seeing and being and, by extension, to render in built form what the British historian Eric Hobsbawm has called "the invention of tradition." Like his political speeches, in which democratic traditions are massaged and molded to taste, the visual culture of Saddam's regime was equally a style marked by pastiche. Pastiche, after all, is the quintessential postmodern form of expression—here put in service of forging a national memory that was a mishmash of Mesopotamian and Islamic eclectica and, increasingly, did a disservice to the formidable history that preceded it.

*   *   *

By the early 2000s, Saddam was the master of a cheerless house. His defeat at the hands of American forces following an unsuccessful invasion of tiny Kuwait damaged the Iraqi morale, leaving it broken and bankrupt. Thirteen years of sanctions didn't help, either, and most of the middle class and intelligentsia who may have profited from Saddam's earlier state-building efforts were long gone. Baghdad was a sad carcass of its former self, and Saddam's paranoia and sense of willful magical realism seemed only to grow by the day. In a 2002 piece in *The Atlantic*, the writer Mark Bowden described Saddam's strenuous efforts, in spite of everything, to radiate strength over this period. To do this, he swam religiously (to keep fit and to mitigate pain from a slipped disc), dyed his hair, and avoided being filmed because of a slight limp (he avoided unscripted walks entirely for fear of being caught on camera looking weak).[8] At the same time, he would deploy ghostwriters in exporting a steady stream of scholarly articles, speeches, and books (all attributed to him). His biography continued to be mandatory reading in school classrooms.

In March of 2003, American coalition forces invaded Iraq on the premise that the country's cache of weapons of mass destruction represented a threat to global security. Just a little over one month later, on May 1, then-President George W. Bush delivered a speech that would come to be known as his "mission accomplished" moment atop the aircraft carrier USS *Abraham Lincoln* (incidentally,

---

[8] Mark Bowden, "Tales of the Tyrant," *The Atlantic Monthly*, May 2002.

he was the first president in history to script a landing on an aircraft carrier in a jet). Bush went on to don a flight suit and pose for photographs with members of the ship's crew before giving a short, uninsightful speech in which he declared the end of major combat operations in Iraq while a banner with the words MISSION ACCOMPLISHED inscribed upon it flapped in the wind behind him. Television cameras cut from beaming George W. to the banner to cheering American servicemen and then long shots of the expanse of the very expensive aircraft carrier. Later, former Secretary of State Donald Rumsfeld would tell the journalist Bob Woodward that he had received an advance copy of that speech and deleted any references to the words "mission accomplished" in its body. He added, "they fixed the speech, but not the sign." The expensive photo-op, assailed from multiple corners for its extraordinary hubris, prevailed.

Months later, as American deaths in Iraq continued to mount, Bush traveled to Iraq to celebrate Thanksgiving with American servicemembers—probably in part to make amends for the disastrously premature declaration of victory some month before. He was, of course, photographed happily eating a turkey, though it was revealed not much later that the turkey might have been made from plastic (the reports remain conflicting on the veracity of the turkey). The writer Naomi Klein

106

Untitled

wrote in *The Nation*: "This was the year when fake-ness ruled: fake rationales for war, a fake President dressed as a fake soldier declaring a fake end to combat and then holding up a fake turkey." Bush, like Saddam before him, had erected his own mag-ical-realist theater in which heady concepts like "democracy" and "the people" were not much more than props — here, rendered in plastic no less.

Just one month earlier, the cameras of the world had focused on Iraqis and American soldiers taking pot shots at a statue of Saddam Hussein in downtown Baghdad's Firdos Square. A small group had gathered around the shameful totem — for the most part unspectacular as a work of art or even agitprop that had been built the year before to celebrate Saddam's sixty-fifth birthday. Some draped an American flag over the unlucky dic-tator's head. As time passed, more and more TV crews and photographers arrived from the nearby Palestine Hotel, a favored watering hotel for mem-bers of the international journalistic glitterati, and eventually, a Marine vehicle pulled down Saddam's head with a crane — an image that was broadcast and rebroadcast before the eyes of the world. Just a few minutes after the toppling, Rumsfeld had this to say: "The scenes of free Iraqis celebrat-ing in the streets, riding American tanks, tearing down the statues of Saddam Hussein in the center of Baghdad are breathtaking. Watching them, one

108

cannot help but think of the fall of the Berlin Wall and the collapse of the Iron Curtain."

Since that fateful toppling—a single image that at least in part came to define the war—some have come forward to argue that it had been a made-for-media manufactured event, with others going as far as to offer that the jubilant Iraqis caught on film were in fact brought in and asked to enact their newfound freedom in this way before the international press corps. Countless blogs featured aerial images of the site, revealing 150 or 200 people hovering like bees in one corner of a vast, mostly empty expanse. Cameras, it seems, had zoomed in on the individuals who had assembled, producing the effect of a crowd. Others offered that the Iraqis present were members of exiled Ahmed Chalabi's "Free Iraq Forces" militia who had been bussed in. Chalabi, as it happens, was a key ally of the American invasion. The alleged staging inspired an 8,851-word investigative piece in *The New Yorker* by Peter Maass. In it, Maass offered:

> Live television loves suspense, especially if it is paired with great visuals. The networks almost never broke away from Firdos Square. The event lived on in replays, too. A 2005 study of CNN's and Fox's coverage, conducted by a research team from

George Washington University and titled "As Goes the Statue, So Goes the War," found that between 11 AM and 8 PM that day Fox replayed the toppling every 4.4 minutes, and CNN every 7.5 minutes. The networks also showed the toppling in house ads; it became a branding device. They continually used the word "historic" to describe the statue's demise.[9]

Like Saddam's deployment of monuments, speeches, and passion plays in the service of his own narratives, the Firdos images performed an important non-truth: the war in Iraq was not just beginning, but rather, had come to an end. Whether the scene was choreographed or not, those images ushered in, once and for all, the end of an era marked by Saddam the artist-leader's ability to groom and define the visual face of Iraq. That end was dramatically underscored some months later as CNN headlines screeched: "Saddam 'Caught Like a Rat' in a Hole." It was December of 2003, and the search for the fallen dictator had come to an end when he was discovered at the bottom of a narrow coffin-sized hole, underneath a shack on a sheep farm about nine miles from Tikrit, his ancestral home. Press

---

[9] Peter Maass, "The Toppling," *The New Yorker*, January 10, 2011.

images revealed a haggard, bearded, and deranged-looking Saddam in theatrical agony. During the press conference announcing his capture, American forces revealed not only the hole in which he was discovered, but images of Saddam undergoing a medical exam, jaws gaping open, military doctors sticking all manner of invasive instruments inside his mouth. A handful of Iraqis in the press conference room emitted celebratory shrieks.

In the meantime, other images proliferated care of the bounty of photojournalists who continued to travel to Iraq, coming to define the visual culture of the war and its aftermath. Especially common were graffitied effigies on Saddam's monuments (in English, of course), buff American troops playing basketball in his vaulted former palaces, along with other image-traces of the former dictator's embarrassing vanities (like his love for *Star Wars*). Before long, the media fixated on the purpled fingers of Iraqi women who had voted in the country's first post-Saddam elections and other subalterns who had regained their dignity following the fall of the dictator. The litany of clichés, sometimes as bad as those of the former leader, were wincingly manufactured for public consumption as the American occupying force would, for the moment at least, be setting the tone for the visual regimes to come.

And then, in December of 2006, a grainy video, care of the cell phone of an individual who was later revealed to be a guard, showed Saddam's hanging death following his conviction for crimes against humanity by the Iraqi Special Tribunal. Wearing a sober black suit over a white shirt, he is chaperoned by ominously hooded men to what look like medieval wooden gallows in a darkened room. Cameras flashing incessantly occasionally light up his face, which, for the most part, seems expressionless. A noose is placed around his neck, and as he falls to his death, some of the assembled taunt him (it is not clear who they are), while others recite the *shahada*. The screen goes black, and after some time, the camera manages to focus in on his (dead) face.

There are hundreds of versions of Saddam's hanging to be found on the Internet, some set to music (perhaps most prominently, Queen's "Another One Bites the Dust"), others with graphics added, and still others accompanied by editorial captions (as in "The Hanging of a Dick Tater!"). In at least one memorable video, a trio of very young Arab boys pretend to re-create the hanging in their home. While it may be hard to envisage what Saddam, should he have survived this period, would have done in the age of the Internet, there is little question that the medium's massively diffuse and DIY nature would have fractured his monopoly on representation sooner than later. Saddam, the man who once filmed the prelude to mass execution in 1979, was not the first leader to understand the

power of images in crafting historical memory —
nor would he be the last — but the era of Saddam
Hussein the visionary architect and artist-leader
had come to an ignoble, if not shocking end. His
monumental Victory Arch had been subsumed into
the fortress-like American-run Green Zone. The
dramatic onion-shaped Monument to the Martyrs
had served as barracks for coalition troops during
the invasion and its aftermath.[10] Iraq's most formidable museums had been looted. And the memory
of the various international avant-gardes who had
visited and worked in Iraq had long faded. The
emperor-leader had lost his clothes, and it was
all there in its entirety for the world to see — on
YouTube, no less.

[10] Antoon, *Middle East Research and Information Project.*

KANT, MILL, HUSSEIN?

Nickolas Calabrese

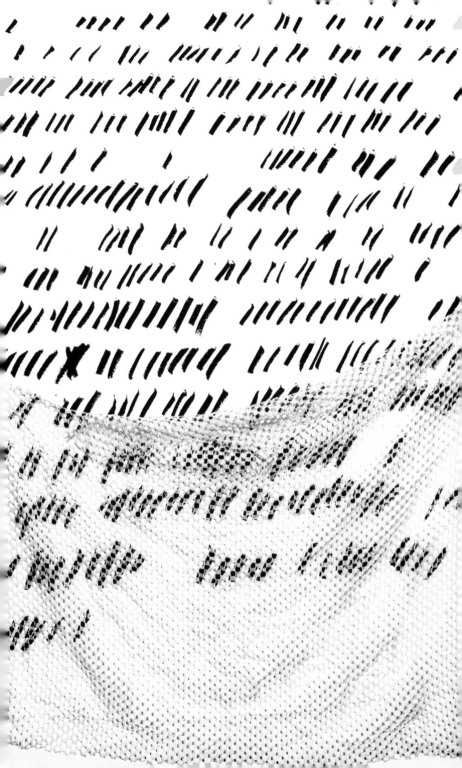

Saddam Hussein (whose given name means "he who confronts" in Arabic) was viewed by opponents as a ruthless dictator, and by his allies as a proponent of pan-Arabism and nationalism who would stop at nothing to strengthen and unite the Arab world, starting with Iraq. In these three early speeches on democracy, which Hussein wrote and delivered in the 1970s as vice-president of Iraq, one would be hard pressed to locate the notorious dictator who rose to power through murder, torture, and blatant human-rights abuse and who waged a genocidal extermination of the Kurds (among many other vile engagements). Hussein's brand of democracy crossed with socialism was singular, but not without its own historical precedents. It is rooted in what he considered to be his fatherly knowledge of his people. This notion of democracy entailed several major anomalies. First, Hussein did not consider democracy to be a system where every citizen of the state has an equal opinion—instead, as he described in these speeches, he would exercise what he considered to be in the best interest of his people, regardless of what it meant for their individual well-being. Second, he neatly conflated democracy with totalitarianism, such that *his* regulation of every aspect of Iraqi society was tautologically deemed to be obviously in the best interest of the state, which superseded the individual. And third, there was his delusion that a "central administrative control" could coexist with a legitimate democracy.

Hussein saw no contradictions in this type of rule; on the contrary, he considered it to be an obvious benefit of his variety of political determination according to his logic of comradely brotherhood. In addition to his devotion to democracy, Hussein also spoke of his devotion to socialism. His socialist roots can be found in the spread of socialist thought throughout the Middle East during and after World War II. He was introduced to socialism by his uncle Khairallah Talfah, who had been an army officer. Hussein was partly raised by his uncle in Baghdad, where he was introduced to Khairallah's socialist and nationalist friends, supporters of Baathist ideologies. It is during this time with Khairallah that Hussein's focus on socialism's success in Iraq developed. To most people, the idea of promoting socialism, democracy, and a totalitarian state all at the same time seems perplexing. And it would be surprising that this type of governing had such a successful run for Hussein for such a long time, save for the myriad of similar examples of authority in other states. It is a definite indication of the inexorable power that rhetoric and propaganda have on societies facing confusion and upheaval. The malleability of political agenda is an easy result of well-worded polemics, as long as they are delivered by a strong personality.

Hussein wrote his speeches as though he were promoting utilitarianism as a normative criterion for a just society in Iraq. While there is no evidence that Hussein was familiar with Western utilitarian philosophy or indeed *any* Western philosophy, his utilitarian outlook echoes in some important structural ways the canonical political and ethical thought of John Stuart Mill. The basic idea behind Mill's utilitarianism is that one must strive to do the most good for the most people, or the least harm to the fewest people.[2] A paradigmatic

---

[1] Shiva Balaghi, *Saddam Hussein: A Biography* (Westport: Greenwood Press, 2006). Khairallah later became a member of Hussein's cabinet, guiding him in socialist practices and policies.

[2] This is, of course, a very reductive account of utilitarian thought, for the sake of brevity. For a more full treatment of utilitarian thought, see John Stuart Mill, *On Liberty*, 1859; John Stuart Mill, *Utilitarianism*, 1863; David Lyons, *Forms and Limits of Utilitarianism*, 1965; John Rawls, *A Theory of Justice*, 1971; and Samuel Scheffler, *The Rejection of Consequentialism*, 1994.

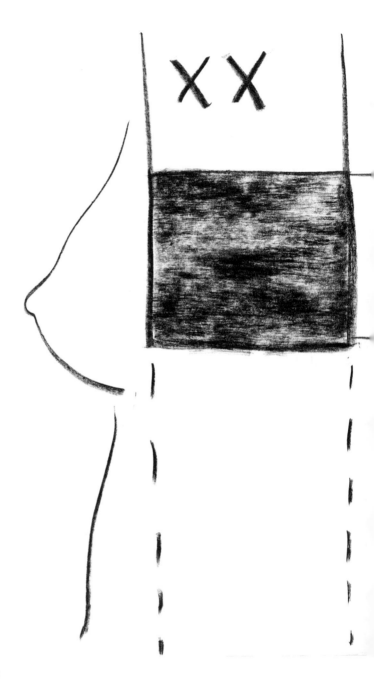

Tally 4

thought experiment that illustrates utilitarian thought (known as the Trolley Problem, and introduced by Philippa Foot) goes loosely as follows: A railroad track splits into two paths; there are five people tied to the track on one path, and on the other path, just one person is tied. The train operator cannot stop in time to avoid killing anyone, but must choose one path or the other: killing one person or killing five people. The utilitarian says that the operator must choose the path with one person, regardless of who that person is: even if, say, it is the train operator's own mother. For the utilitarian, if killing one person saves five lives, that act is morally necessary.

To take the decision of doing the greatest good for the greatest number of people to such an extreme example of killing one person to save others is kind of at the heart of Hussein's speeches. There is an always-present tendency in them to convince Iraqis that they are all equals in the domain of the state, and that in order to protect the state that grants them equality, they must be willing to go to any lengths to protect it. Hussein's form of utilitarianism is tightly intertwined with this idea of martyrdom. He would always point to the idea that in putting society before self, one should be willing to die in order to preserve Iraq's autonomy. The Trolley Problem clearly exhibits this same ethos: in order to protect the whole of Iraq, its members must be willing to martyr themselves for it. The only problem is that, in Hussein's speeches, the whole of society is usually synonymous with the government of society, which slightly betrays the classic notion of utilitarianism through his vague referencing.

In "Democracy: A Source of Strength for the Individual and Society" (1977), Hussein makes the case that doing the greatest good for the greatest number of people is most effective when choosing pro-society measures over conflicting personal dogmas:

> Whenever family unity conflicts with the proposed policies that are applied to build up the new society, this conflict must be solved in favor of the policies and traditions for building up the new society and not vice versa.

He clearly desired that society as a whole—the Iraqi society—should be the priority. Personal *disagreements* only serve to satisfy the person disagreeing, whereas *agreement* with societal mandates and norms serve to satisfy society as whole. Mill argues similarly when he describes the compromise of one's own values in favor of society's values:

Laws and social arrangements should place the happiness, or (as speaking practically it may be called) the interest, of every individual, as nearly as possible in harmony with the interest of the whole; and . . . education and opinion, which have so vast a power over human character, should so use that power as to establish in the mind of every individual an indissoluble association between his own happiness and the good of the whole.[3]

For Hussein, however, loyalty is not enough to fully satisfy society. One must hand oneself over to martyrdom if the revolution necessitates it. Martyrdom is generally a concept more verbalized in Eastern cultures than in Western cultures, though it does have precedent in both. While Mill probably would not have used the actual term "martyrdom" in his philosophy, he still flirts with notions of martyrdom. Just as Hussein suggests martyrdom as the most morally pure choice when given the decision, Mill interestingly suggests the same, though he relies on the more Western concept and terminology of sacrifice. He makes a clear claim that some generations

---

[3] John Stuart Mill, *Utilitarianism and Other Essays* (New York: Penguin Books Inc., 1987), 288–89.

may suffer in order to gain a better society as a whole in the future:

> All the grand sources, in short, of human suffering are in a great degree, many of them almost entirely, conquerable by human care and effort . . . though their removal is grievously slow—though a long succession of generations will perish in the breach before the conquest is completed.[4]

It is interesting to note that Mill stresses education as a way toward liberation from selfish behavior. Hussein makes much the same case in his "Source of Strength" speech, stating that loyalty and unity should be maintained from an early age through the national education system.

Hussein also implanted an extraordinary sense of duty into his speeches, and the duty to do one's part in advancing society is paramount. The role of duty seems pretty obvious even from a brief reading of Hussein's speeches, but again, illuminating precedent for the relation of duty to more individual wishes can be found in the traditions of Western moral and political philosophy. Immanuel Kant, notably, believed that duty to do the morally

---

[4] Ibid., 286–87.

just thing was part of a rational being's difficult path to enlightenment, and probably involved a bit of cognitive dissonance in arriving there. He believed that reason is a practical faculty meant to *produce* a good will and *influence* it; and the will is merely the condition for good in all other faculties. As he explicates in the *Foundations of the Metaphysics of Morals*:

> The thought of duty and of the moral law generally, with no admixture of empirical inducements, has an influence on the human heart so much more powerful than all other incentives which may be derived from the empirical field that reason, in the consciousness of its dignity, despises them and gradually becomes master over them. It has this influence only through reason alone, which thereby first realizes that it can of itself be practical.[5]

Kant takes this conception of duty through reason as something for which an agent should always aim, especially when it conflicts with one's personal

[5] Immanuel Kant, Selections: *Foundations of the Metaphysics of Morals*, ed. Lewis White Beck (Englewood Cliffs, NJ: Prentice Hall, 1988), 260–61.

values. For Kant, only one's *will* could be considered to be good. He thought that the good will has a sort of immanence that is unique to it. Therefore if one makes a decision to sacrifice oneself in order to save a greater number of people, one is acting in a morally good way. The will should act out of duty, and it should come from within each person.

In declaring the nationalist duty to be superlative for each person, Hussein conflated the Kantian ideal of duty with the nationalist ideal of martyrdom for the state. It should also be noted that Mill was influenced by the Kantian sense of duty: Mill says that it is not necessary "to decide whether the feeling of duty is innate or implanted," though he does admit to believing that "moral feelings are not innate, but acquired" through a good education of what is just for society and what is unjust.[6] Both Western and Eastern ideals of morality necessitate duty (think of individuals enlisting in the military in order to protect their country), along with freedom of the will to make morally just choices. Loyalty and freedom, for Hussein, are two aspects of the same thing (moral decision-making), such that if one is free then one must be loyal to the state for that freedom. Remarkably, Kant and Mill would both probably subscribe to similar positions regarding morality's entailment of freedom to act dutifully loyal.

---

[6] Mill, *Utilitarianism and Other Essays*, 302.

Hussein's speech "One Trench or Two?," which he delivered to the National Assembly in 1976, perfectly displays the propensity toward duty. In it Hussein argues that it is every Iraqi's duty to support the whole of Iraq, even if it means disregarding the urge to publicly show disapproval of governmental policy. (On the other hand, in "A Source of Strength," Saddam exhorts parents to teach their children to "criticize their parents politely if they heard them talk about the secrets of Party organizations"; each son "would receive his directives from the Revolution's responsible center and carry them out . . . while he maintains and respects family unity.") With recommendations that Iraqis should publically show support of the Baathists (even if they dissent viscerally), Hussein advocated his inflexible belief in nationalistic duty. That everyone should be of the same opinion when considering Iraq's official stance is assumed by Hussein in the speech. Maintaining an efficient and just society leaves no other alternative than allegiance to what the majority party supports—his party, of course.

Hussein calls on all Arabs to embody this sense of duty in everything from withstanding pressures by Western states, to resisting bourgeois ways, to identifying Arabs as superior. This in part is what led Hussein to being viewed as a leader not only to Iraq but to all Arab peoples. His wide-ranging support lasted from before his presidency began

Untitled

in 1979 until after his execution. Indeed, riots erupted all over the Middle East in response to Hussein's execution in December of 2006. Until the end of his life he remained deeply committed to the nationalist and socialist polemics of his early speeches. When he was sentenced to death, Hussein stood up in the courtroom and shouted in defiance, "Long live the people! Long live the Arab nation!"[7]

Hussein probably understood how his arguments conflicted with many of the things he did. But he probably did believe he was acting democratically with a simultaneous totalitarianism. It is a good bet, given the tone displayed in his speeches, that he willfully misunderstood democracy. It is definite that he wrote them in order to secure his followers, and to persuade others to join the Baath party. But dictators have historically produced writings that overlook their actions and celebrate their beliefs, and the goal has always been the same: to hold onto the power that they fought hard to attain. His musings on democracy thus had a practical application. In "Democracy: A Principled and Practical Necessity" (1978), he wrote, "Interaction with the people's public life and respect of the people's opinion have become a fact, receiving growing attention from peoples of the world. The authorities

---

[7] Kirk Semple, "Saddam Hussein is Sentenced to Death," *New York Times* (November 5, 2006).

derive their powers from it." Hussein made clear that *his democracy* was different from *democracy*, because it could coexist with central authoritative control, and he knew this to fly in the face of *democracy*. He wrote tellingly in "A Source of Strength," "There is nothing more dangerous than a human being who feels he is wronged, because he will turn into a huge explosive force when he feels that no one in the State or in society is on his side to redress the injustice." Indeed Hussein *did* exercise control as a treacherous leader, and his speeches certainly had some successful determination in the length of his reign. In 1978 alone about three million copies of nineteen speeches authored by Hussein were printed and distributed among Iraq's citizens.[8] It is their efficacy that makes these propagandistic documents so important for the world to understand, both Westerners and Easterners, because political injustice can happen anywhere under any name. The transformation of democracy into any type of oppressive political system can be a matter of a few well-spoken words.

---

[8] Shiva Balaghi, *Saddam Hussein*.

CONTRIBUTORS

NEGAR AZIMI is senior editor of *Bidoun* magazine. She has written for *Artforum*, *Frieze*, *Harper's*, and *The New York Times Magazine*, among other venues. She sits on the boards of the Beirut-based Arab Image Foundation, and Artists Space in New York.

NICKOLAS CALABRESE is an artist and writer who lives and works in New York. He is currently working on a project exploring the relationship of trolling to art and philosophy.

PAUL CHAN is an artist who lives and works in New York. Recent exhibitions include *dOCUMENTA (13)*, Kassel, 2012; *Before The Law*, Ludwig Museum, Cologne, 2011–12; and *Making Worlds, 53rd Venice Biennale*, Venice, 2009.

JEFF SEVERNS GUNTZEL has reported from the Middle East and the US as a staff writer for *National Catholic Reporter* and *Village Voice Media*. He was a contributing editor at *Punk Planet* magazine and senior editor at *Utne Reader*. Before journalism, he spent years doing humanitarian work in prewar Iraq. Electronic Iraq, a website he co-founded in 2003 to document the Iraqi experience of war, is archived in the Library of Congress and the British Library.

ACKNOWLEDGMENTS

A book is a book only when it is also a series of relationships that make it worth making. I want to thank Dakis Joannou and the DESTE Foundation for having the interest—and the courage—to co-publish this book. *On Democracy by Saddam Hussein* also would not have been made without Karen Marta, who has played so many roles: editor, taskmaster, advisor, friend. Special thanks to Nell McClister for her astute editing and guidance. Also a special thanks to Chad Kloepfer and Jeff Ramsey of Kloepfer-Ramsey for their superb design of the book. I want to acknowledge Elizabeth Karp-Evans and Dustin Cosentino for their production assistance. The support from Carol Greene, Alexandra Tuttle, Martha Fleming-Ives, and the rest of the staff of Greene Naftali Gallery for the care and documentation of the artwork in this book was invaluable. I am grateful for the great and dedicated crew at Badlands Unlimited. I want to thank Ian Cheng, Micaela Durand, and Madeline Davis for working with me on this book, and so many others that Badlands publishes. This book is also not possible without the support of the people behind Distributed Art Publishers (DAP). They include Todd Bradway, Luke Brown, Alexander Galán, and Elisa Leshowitz. A personal thanks to Marlo Poras and Ruby Chan, who keep me huggin' and thuggin'. Lastly, there is literally no book without the contributors who grace these pages. So my deepest thanks to Negar Azimi, Nickolas Calabrese, and Jeff Severns Guntzel for their writings. Especially Jeff. In 2002, as we sat in a rundown Mexican restaurant in Chicago, Jeff convinced me to join him and other members of the anti-sanctions, antiwar group Voices in the Wilderness on an illegal trip to Baghdad before the second Gulf War. We wanted to stop a war before it began. We failed, of course, but the experience of working with the activists and citizens of Iraq on the eve of the US invasion forever changed how I practice what we call politics. It is still changing, as all living forms ought to. And I have Jeff and Voices to thank for that.

—Paul Chan

135

All images courtesy
of the artist and
Greene Naftali Gallery,
New York.

136